FOR ORGANS, PIANOS & ELECTRONIC KEYBOARDS

E-Z PLAY® TODAY

149

MUSIC FROM THE MOTION PICTURE SOUNDTRACK

2   **All Is Found**

12   **Some Things Never Change**

5   **Into the Unknown**

20   **When I Am Older**

23   **Reindeer(s) Are Better Than People (Cont.)**

24   **Lost in the Woods**

29   **Show Yourself**

36   **The Next Right Thing**

ISBN 978-1-5400-8372-2

Motion Picture Artwork TM & Copyright © 2019 Disney

Visit Hal Leonard Online at
www.halleonard.com

Contact us:
Hal Leonard
7777 West Bluemound Road
Milwaukee, WI 53213
Email: info@halleonard.com

In Europe, contact:
Hal Leonard Europe Limited
42 Wigmore Street
Marylebone, London, W1U 2RN
Email: info@halleonardeurope.com

In Australia, contact:
Hal Leonard Australia Pty. Ltd.
4 Lentara Court
Cheltenham, Victoria, 3192 Australia
Email: info@halleonard.com.au

All Is Found

Registration 4
Rhythm: Pop or Ballad

Music and Lyrics by Kristen Anderson-Lopez
and Robert Lopez

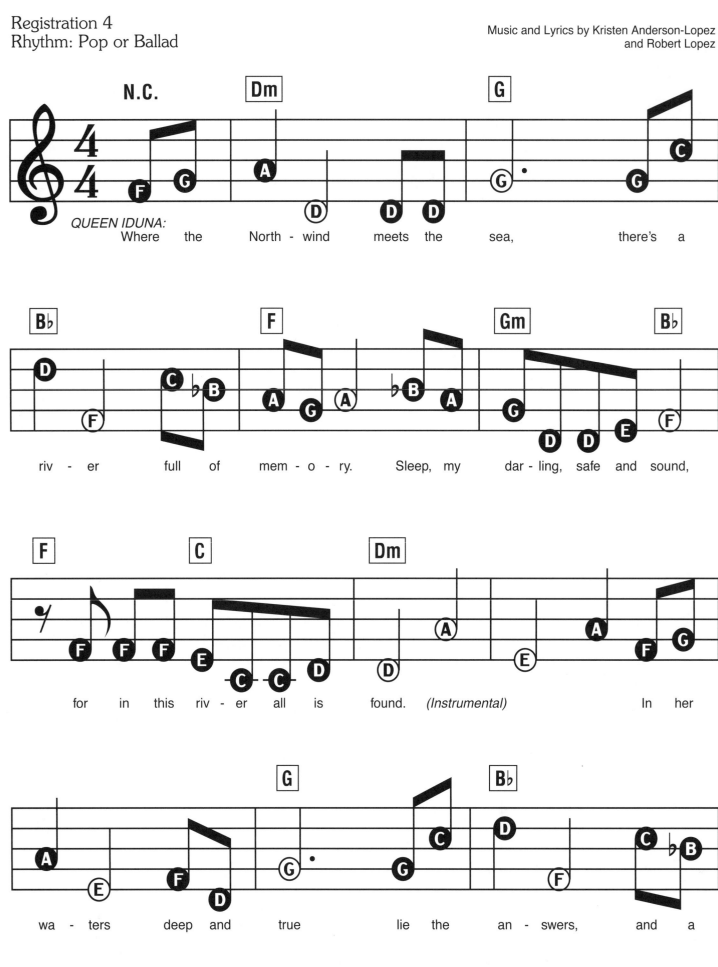

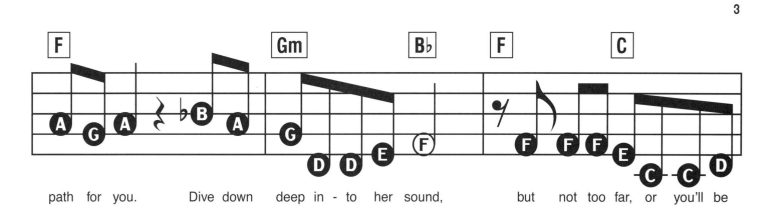

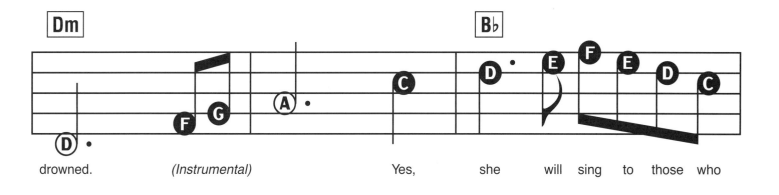

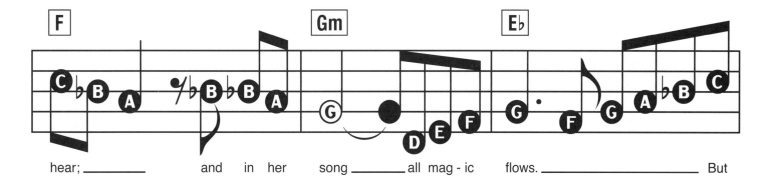

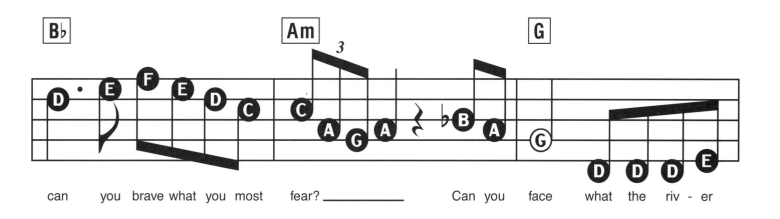

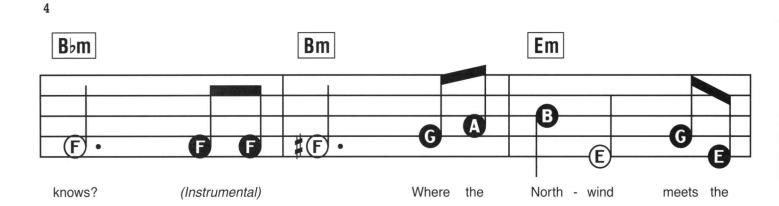

knows? (Instrumental) Where the North - wind meets the

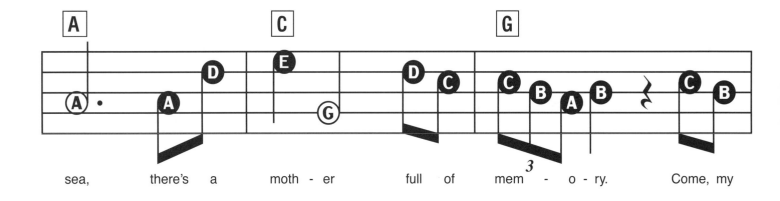

sea, there's a moth - er full of mem - o - ry. Come, my

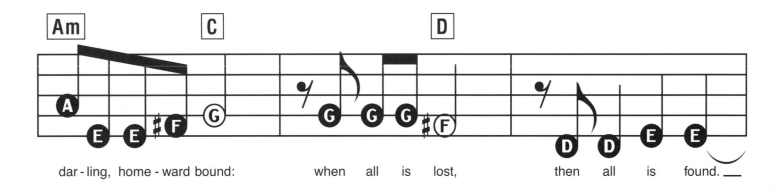

dar - ling, home - ward bound: when all is lost, then all is found. ___

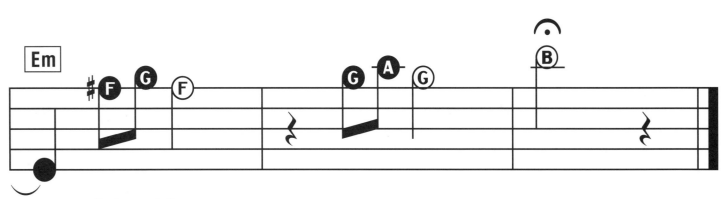

___ (Instrumental)

Into the Unknown

Registration 2
Rhythm: 6/8 March

Music and Lyrics by Kristen Anderson-Lopez
and Robert Lopez

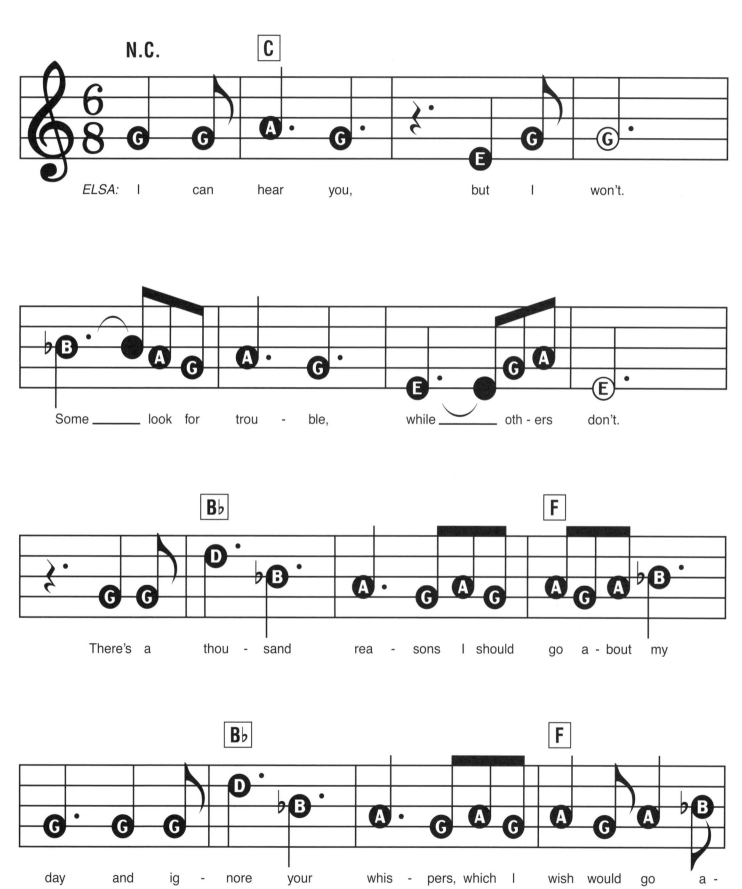

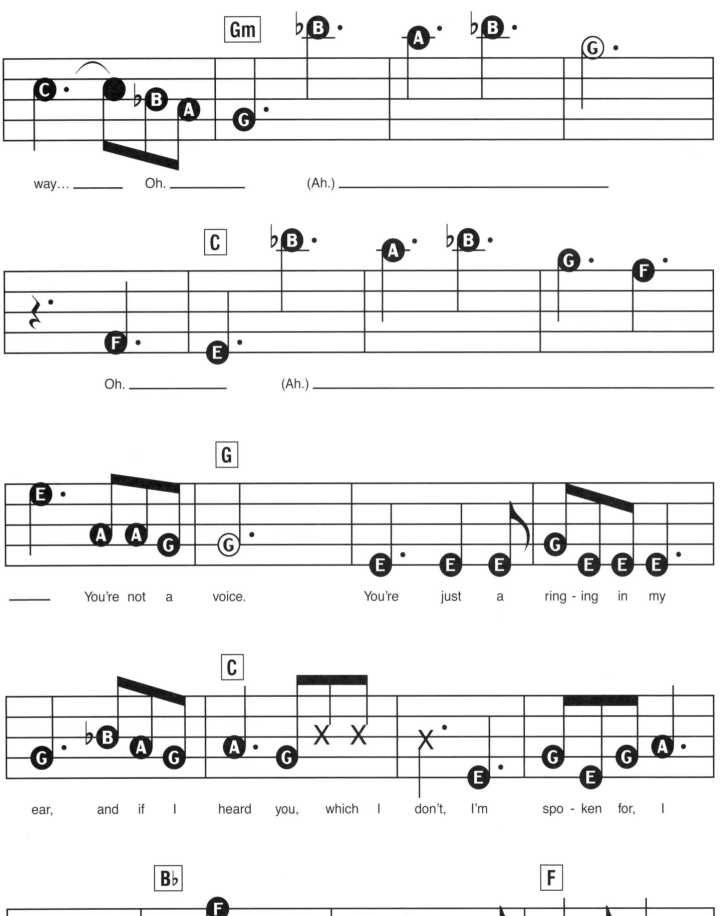

way… _____ Oh. _____ (Ah.) _____

Oh. _____ (Ah.) _____

_____ You're not a voice. You're just a ring-ing in my

ear, and if I heard you, which I don't, I'm spo-ken for, I

fear. Ev-'ry-one I've ev-er loved is here with-in these

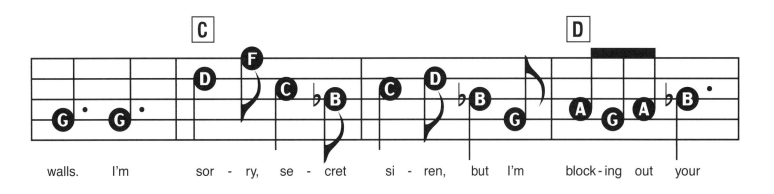

C · G · G · D F C ♭B C D ♭B G D A G A ♭B ·

walls. I'm sor - ry, se - cret si - ren, but I'm block - ing out your

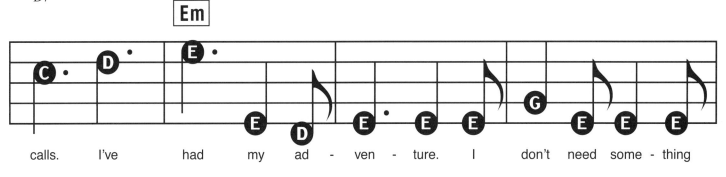

D7

Em

C · D · E · E D E · E E G E E E

calls. I've had my ad - ven - ture. I don't need some - thing

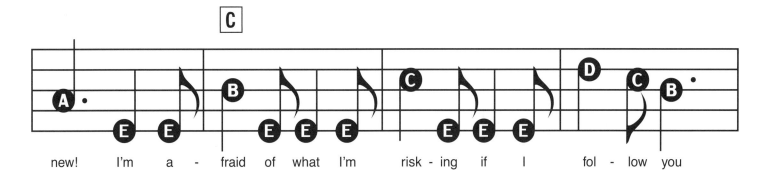

C

A · E E B E E E C E E E D C B ·

new! I'm a - fraid of what I'm risk - ing if I fol - low you

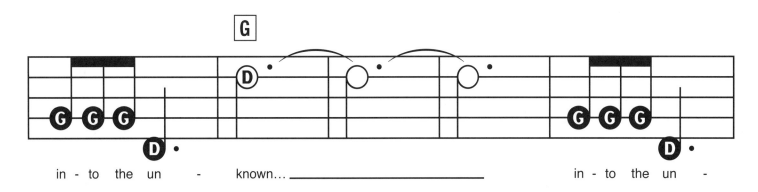

G

G G G D · D · G G G D ·

in - to the un - known... in - to the un -

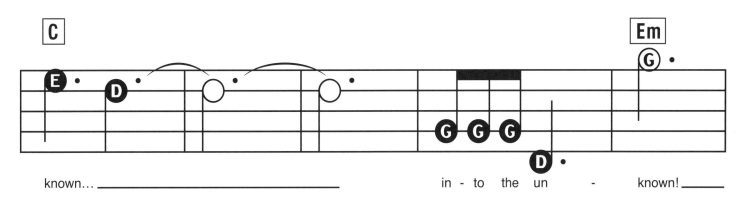

C

Em

E · D · G G G G · D

known... in - to the un - known!

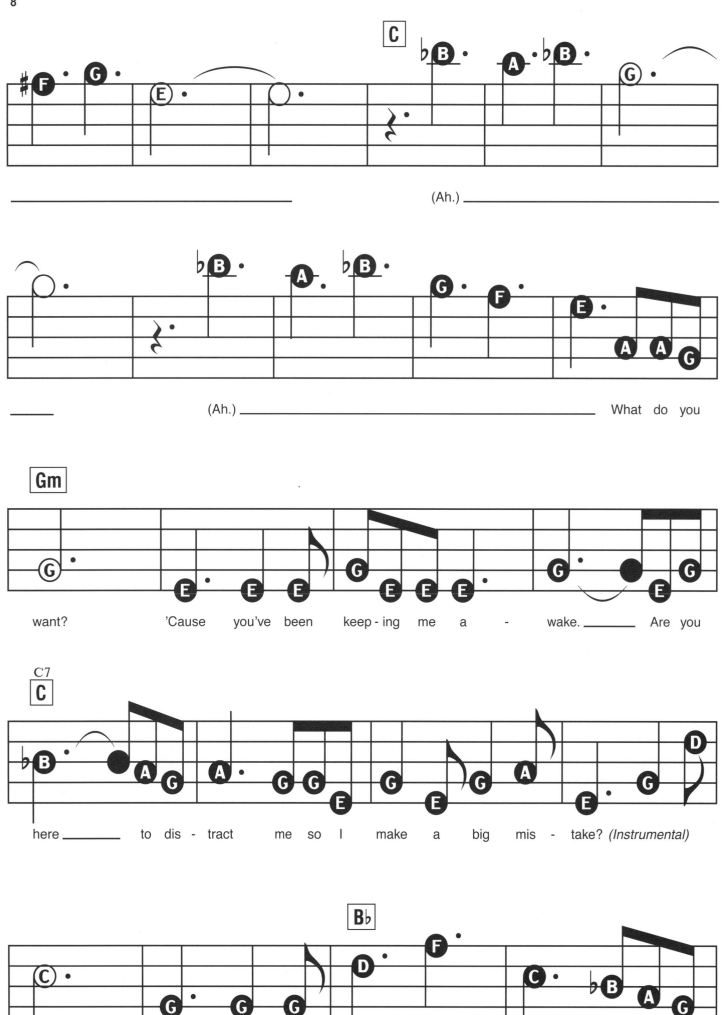

(Ah.)

(Ah.) What do you

want? 'Cause you've been keep-ing me a - wake. _____ Are you

here _____ to dis - tract me so I make a big mis - take? *(Instrumental)*

Or are you some - one out there who's a

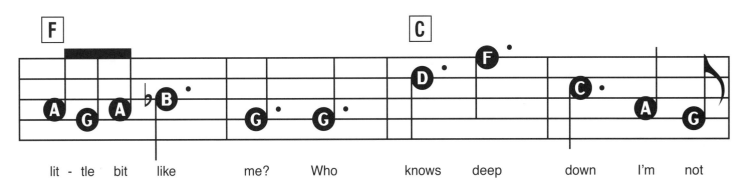

lit - tle bit like me? Who knows deep down I'm not

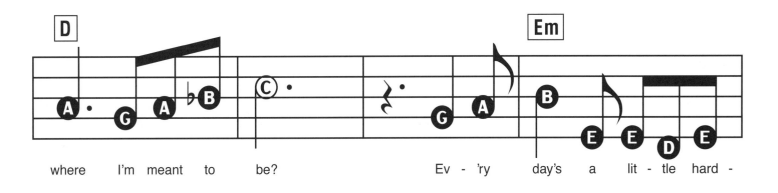

where I'm meant to be? Ev - 'ry day's a lit - tle hard -

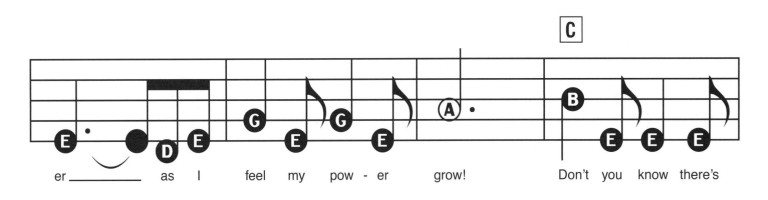

er _____ as I feel my pow - er grow! Don't you know there's

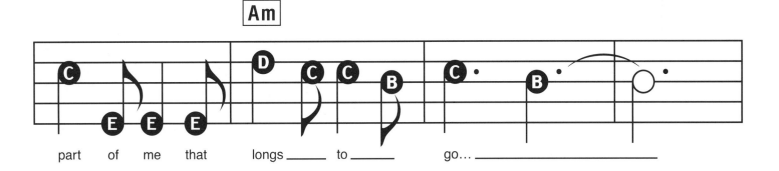

part of me that longs _____ to _____ go...

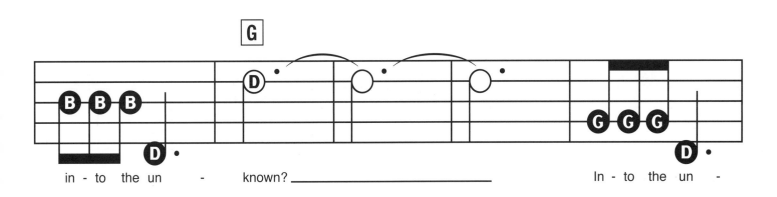

in - to the un - known? _____ In - to the un -

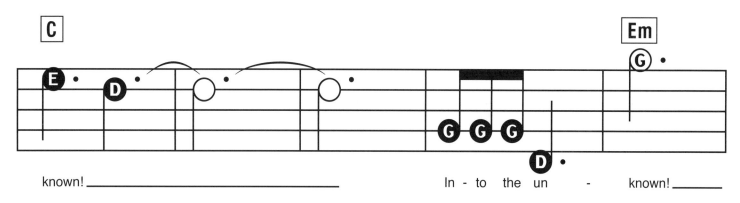

known! _____ In - to the un - known! _____

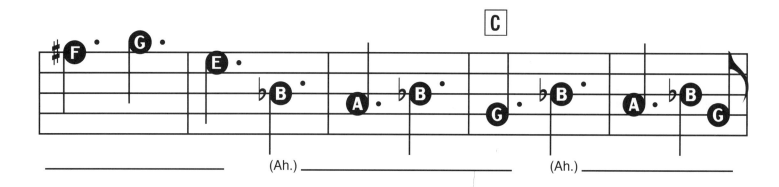

_____ (Ah.) _____ (Ah.) _____

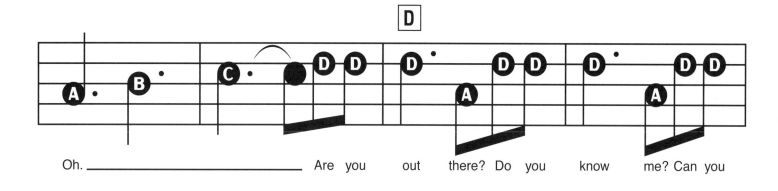

Oh. _____ Are you out there? Do you know me? Can you

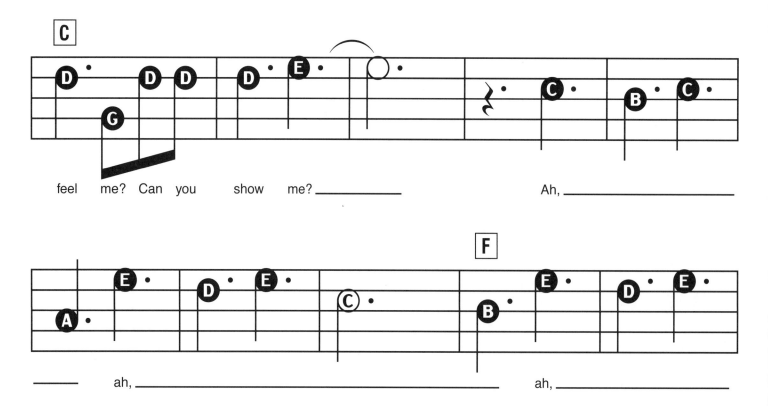

feel me? Can you show me? _____ Ah, _____

_____ ah, _____ ah, _____

11

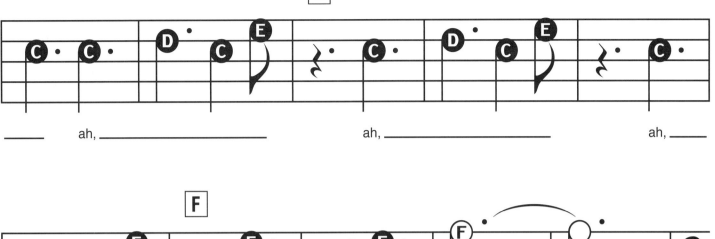

ah, _____ ah, _____ ah, _____

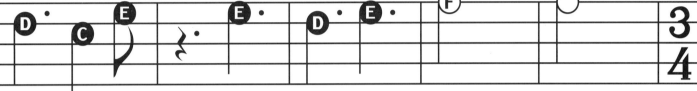

_____ ah, _____

Rhythm: None

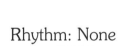

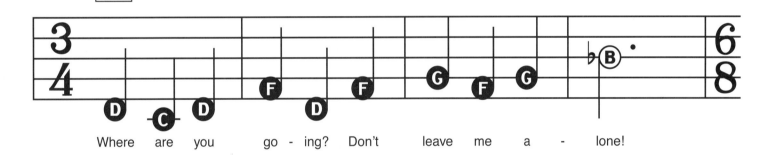

Where are you go - ing? Don't leave me a - lone!

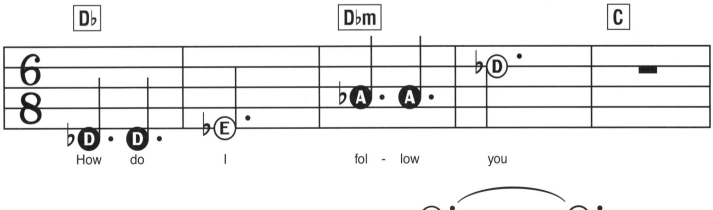

How do I fol - low you

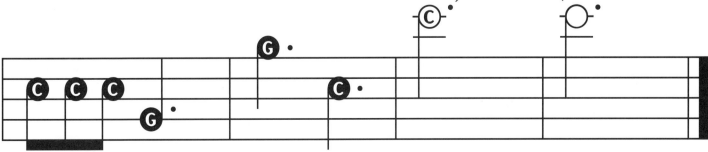

in - to the un - known? *(Instrumental)*

Some Things Never Change

Registration 4
Rhythm: Rock or Pop

Music and Lyrics by Kristen Anderson-Lopez
and Robert Lopez

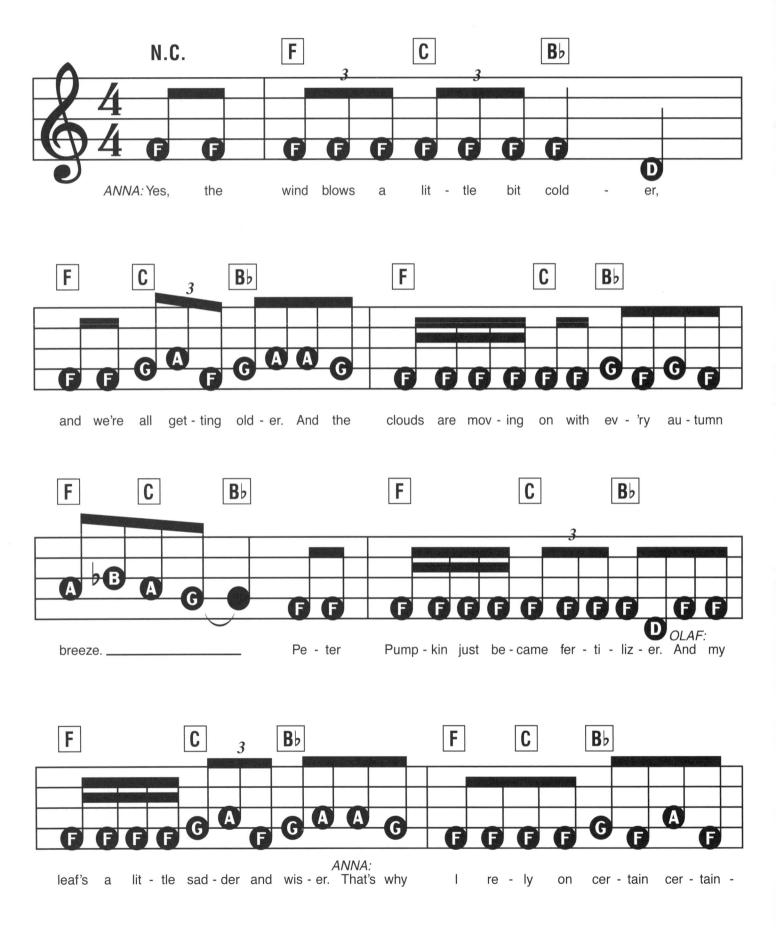

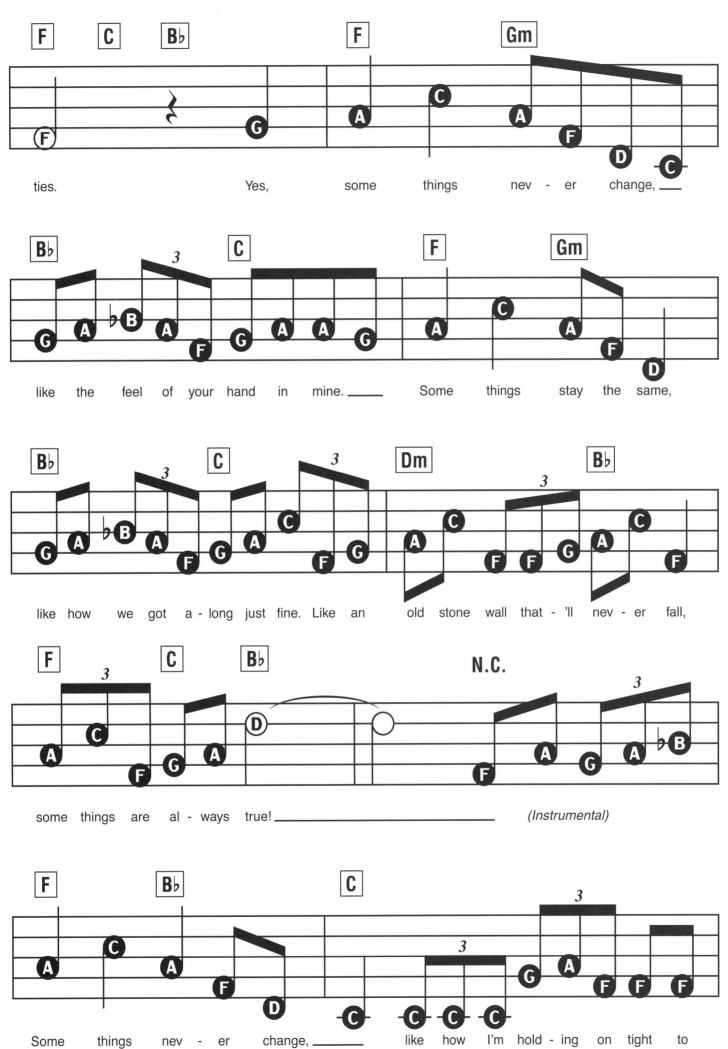

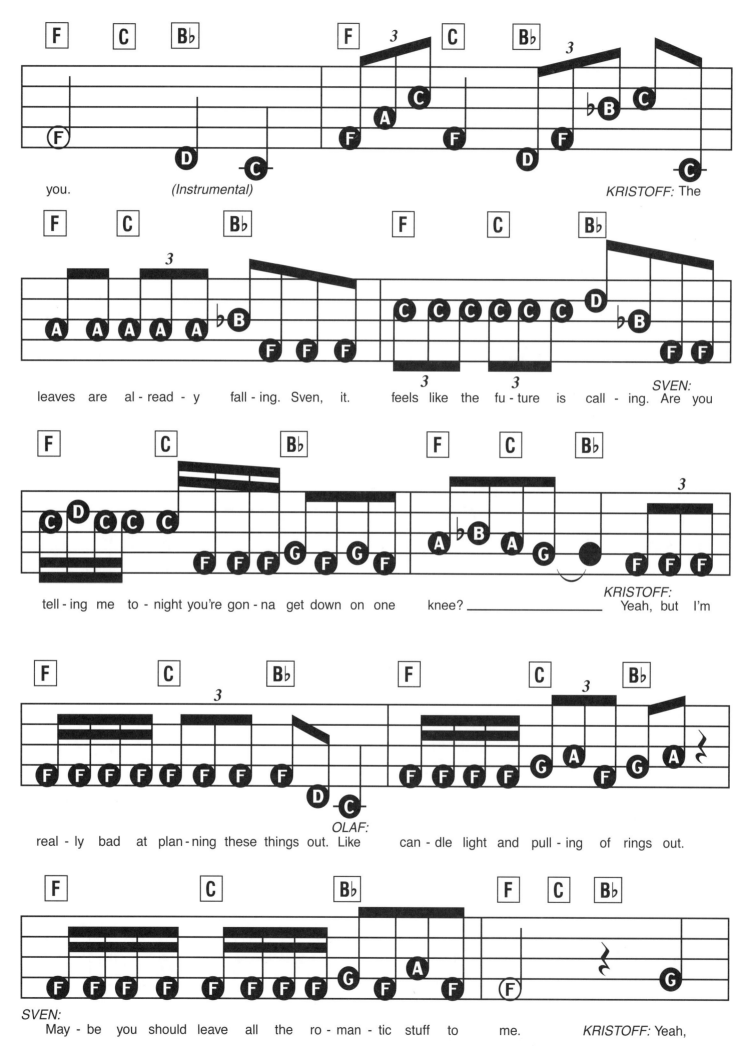

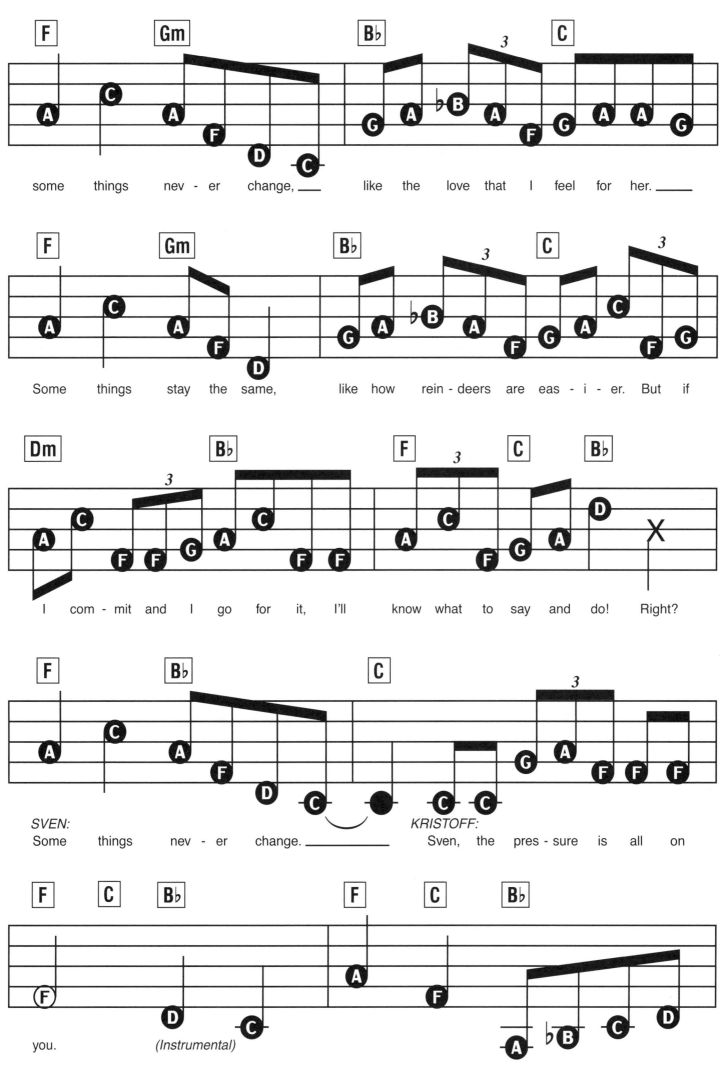

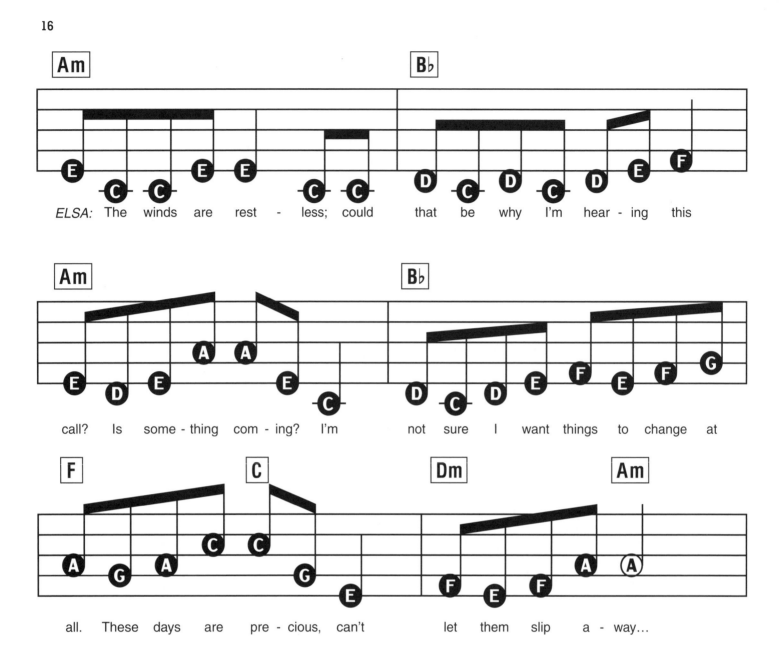

ELSA: The winds are rest - less; could that be why I'm hear - ing this

call? Is some - thing com - ing? I'm not sure I want things to change at

all. These days are pre - cious, can't let them slip a - way…

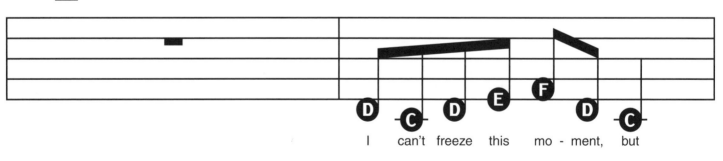

I can't freeze this mo - ment, but

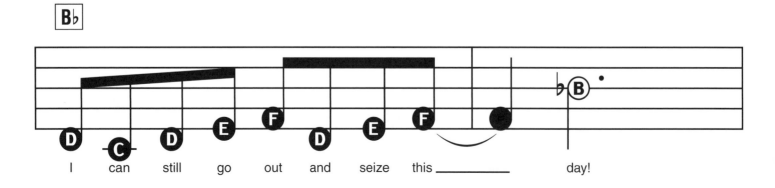

I can still go out and seize this _____ day!

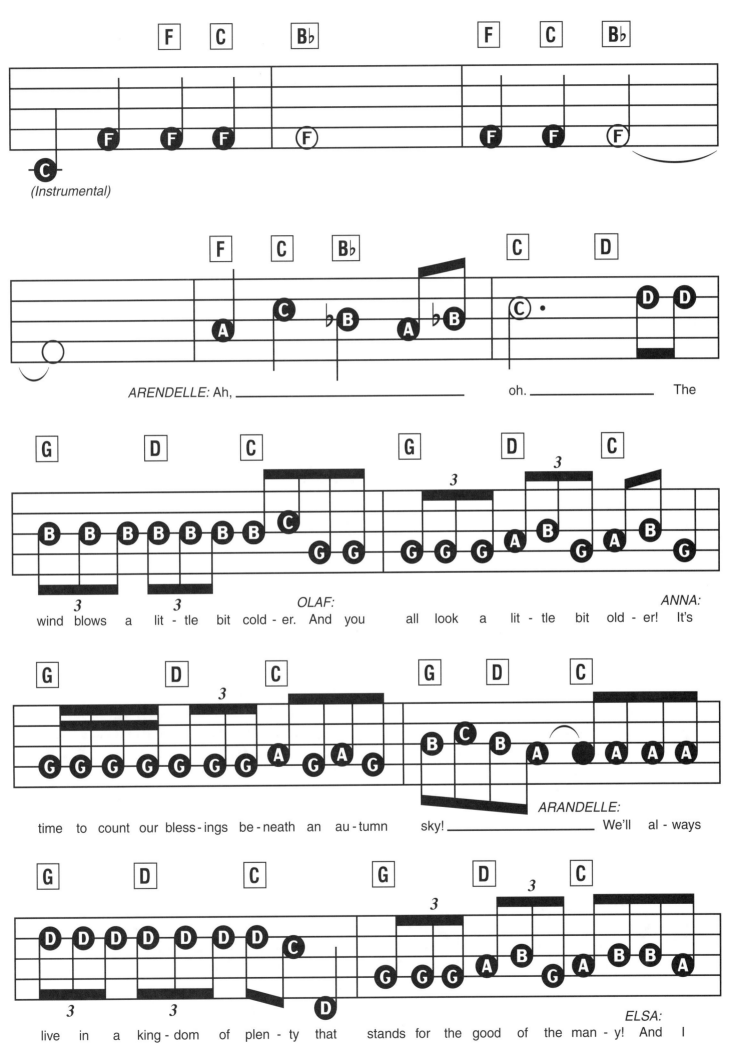

(Instrumental)

ARENDELLE: Ah, _____ oh. _____ The

OLAF:

ANNA:

wind blows a lit - tle bit cold - er. And you all look a lit - tle bit old - er! It's

ARANDELLE:

time to count our bless - ings be - neath an au - tumn sky! _____ We'll al - ways

ELSA:

live in a king - dom of plen - ty that stands for the good of the man - y! And I

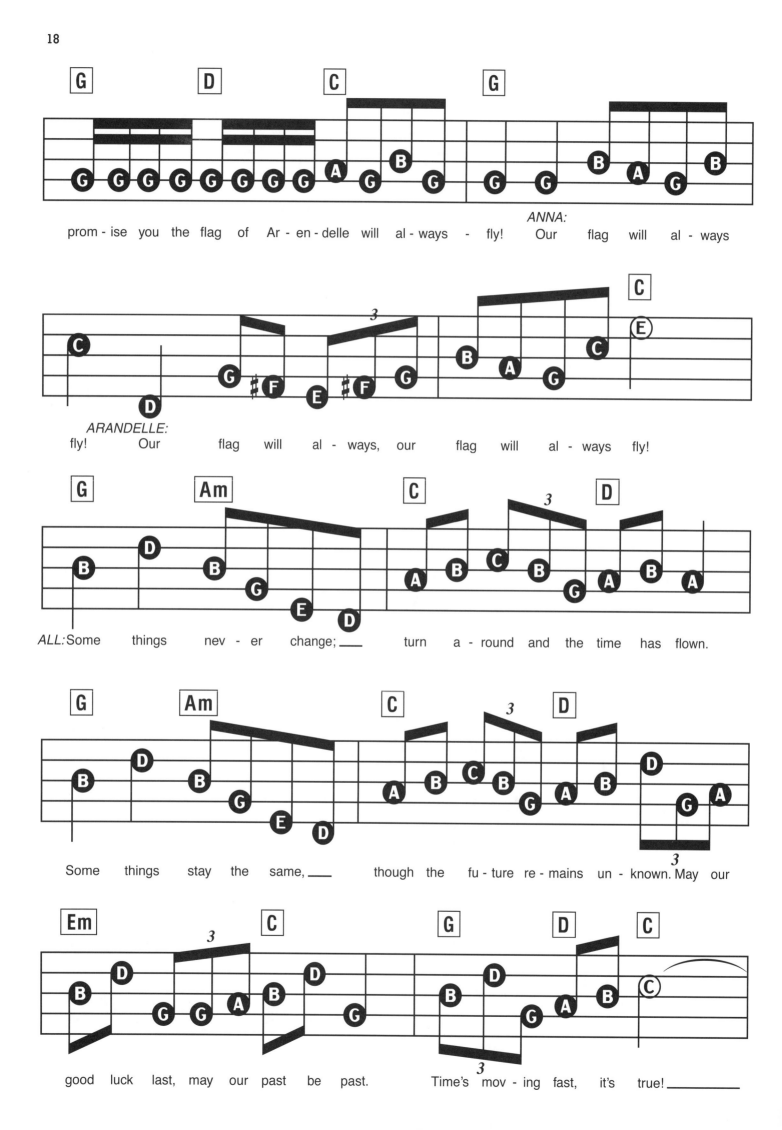

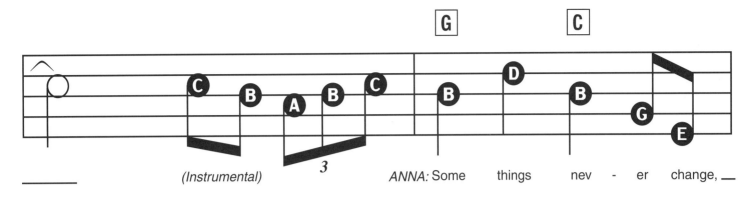

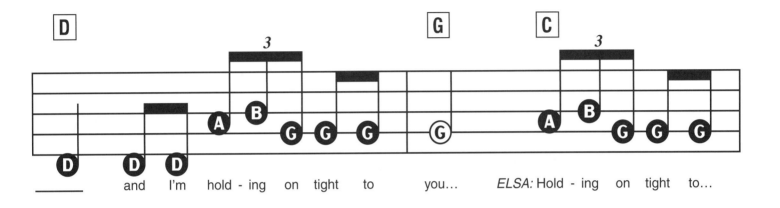

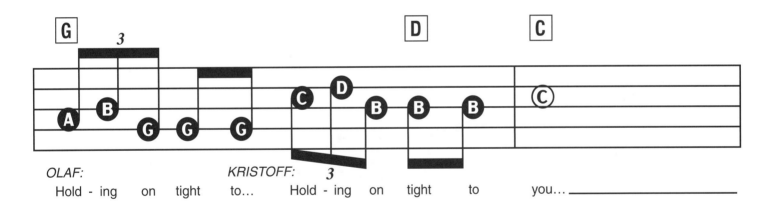

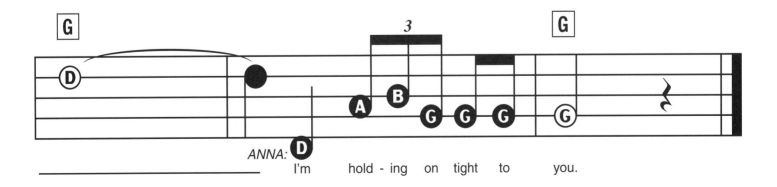

When I Am Older

Registration 9
Rhythm: Swing

Music and Lyrics by Kristen Anderson-Lopez
and Robert Lopez

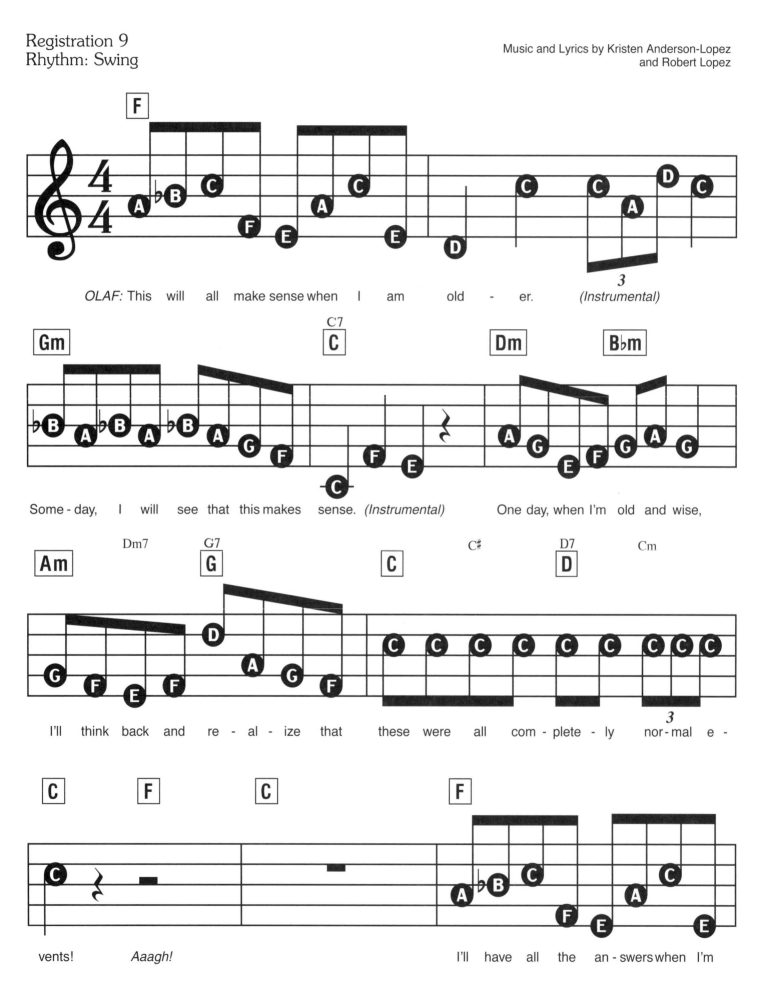

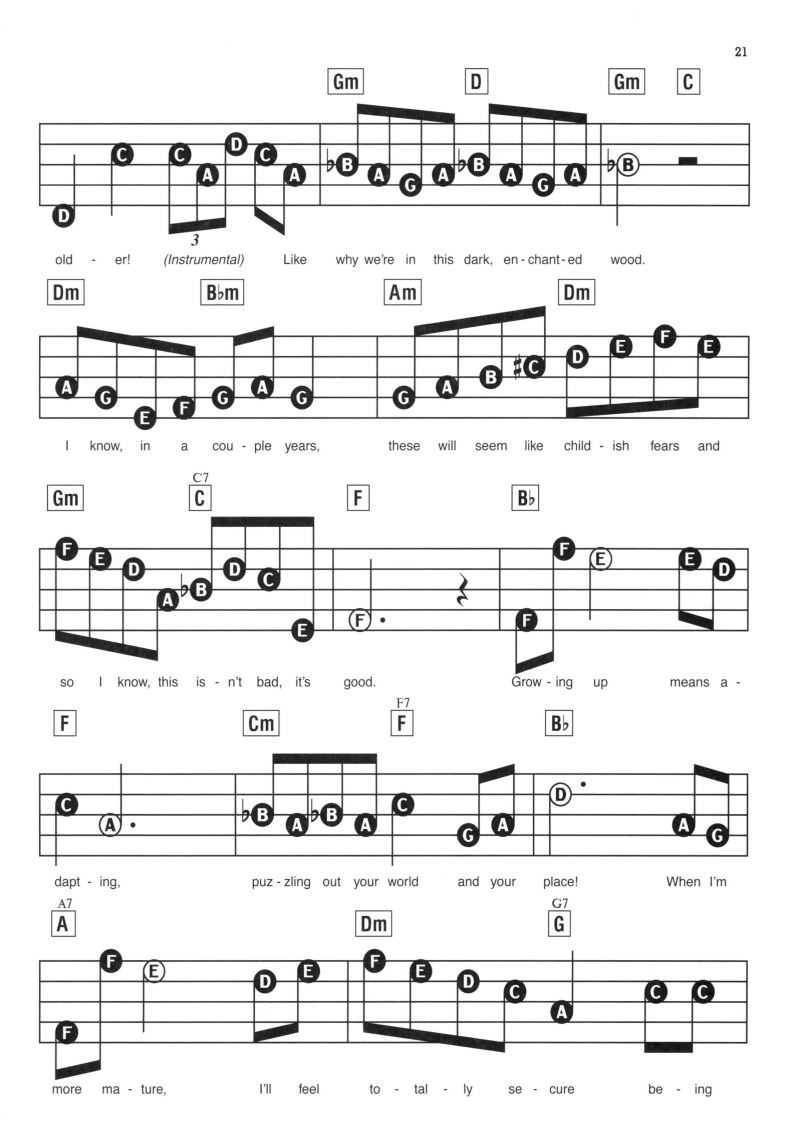

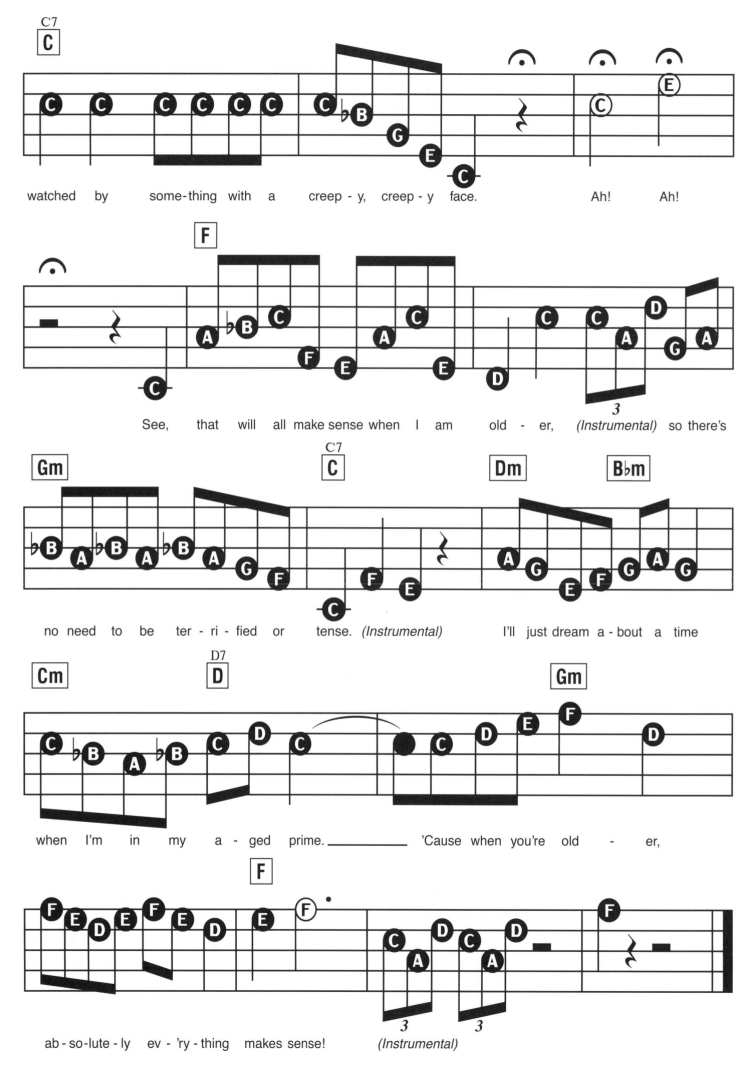

watched by some-thing with a creep-y, creep-y face. Ah! Ah!

See, that will all make sense when I am old-er, (Instrumental) so there's

no need to be ter-ri-fied or tense. (Instrumental) I'll just dream a-bout a time

when I'm in my a-ged prime._____ 'Cause when you're old-er,

ab-so-lute-ly ev-'ry-thing makes sense! (Instrumental)

Reindeer(s) Are Better Than People (Cont.)

Registration 3
Rhythm: None

Music and Lyrics by Kristen Anderson-Lopez
and Robert Lopez

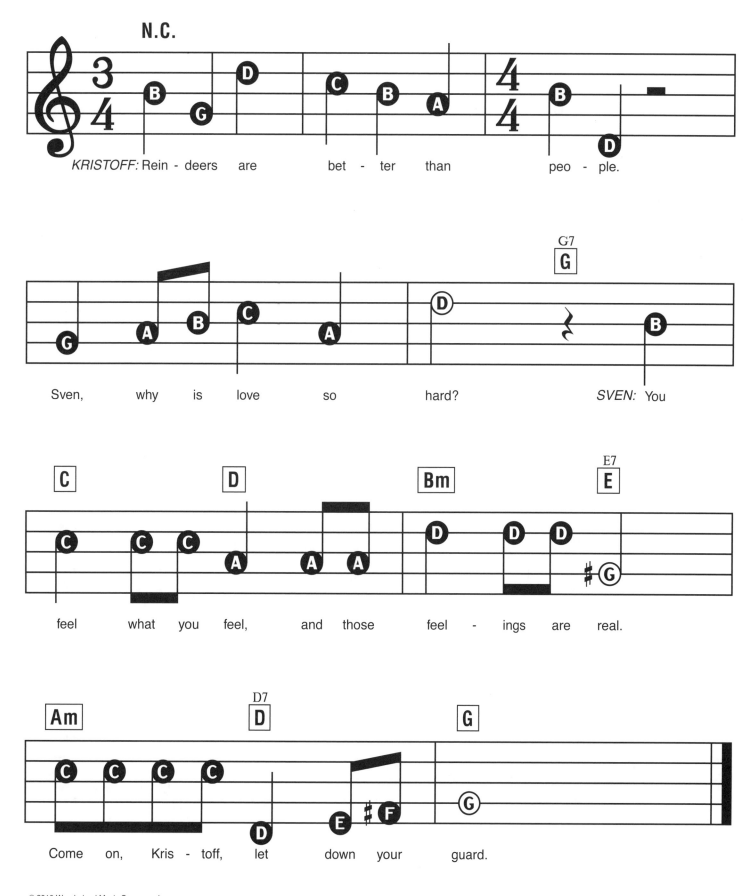

Lost in the Woods

Registration
Rhythm: Pop or Rock

Music and Lyrics by Kristen Anderson-Lopez
and Robert Lopez

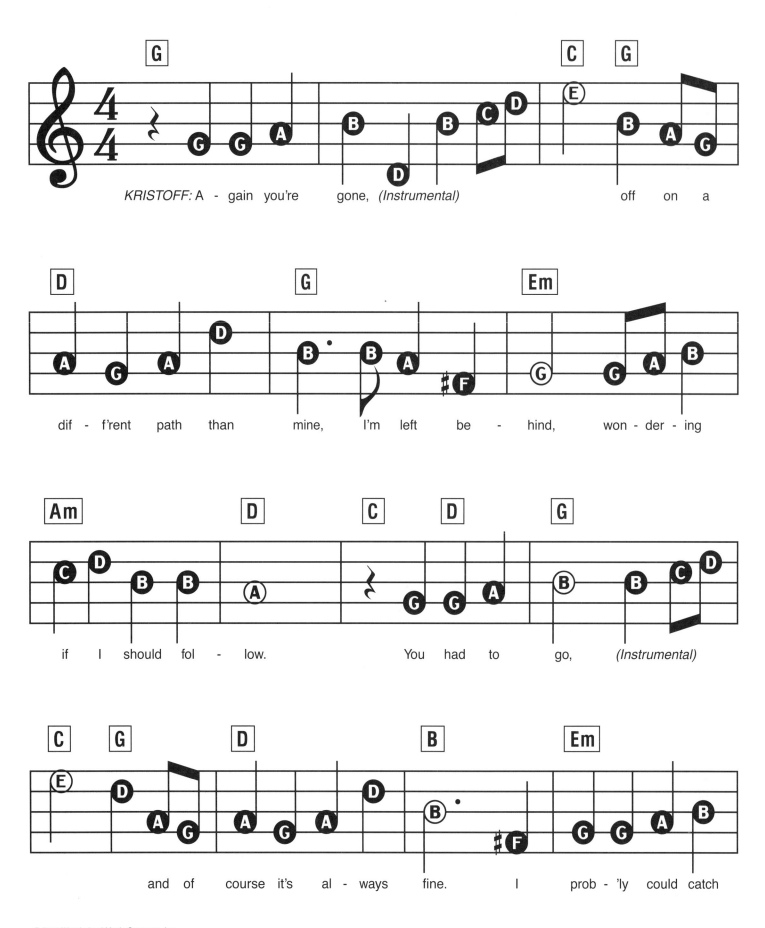

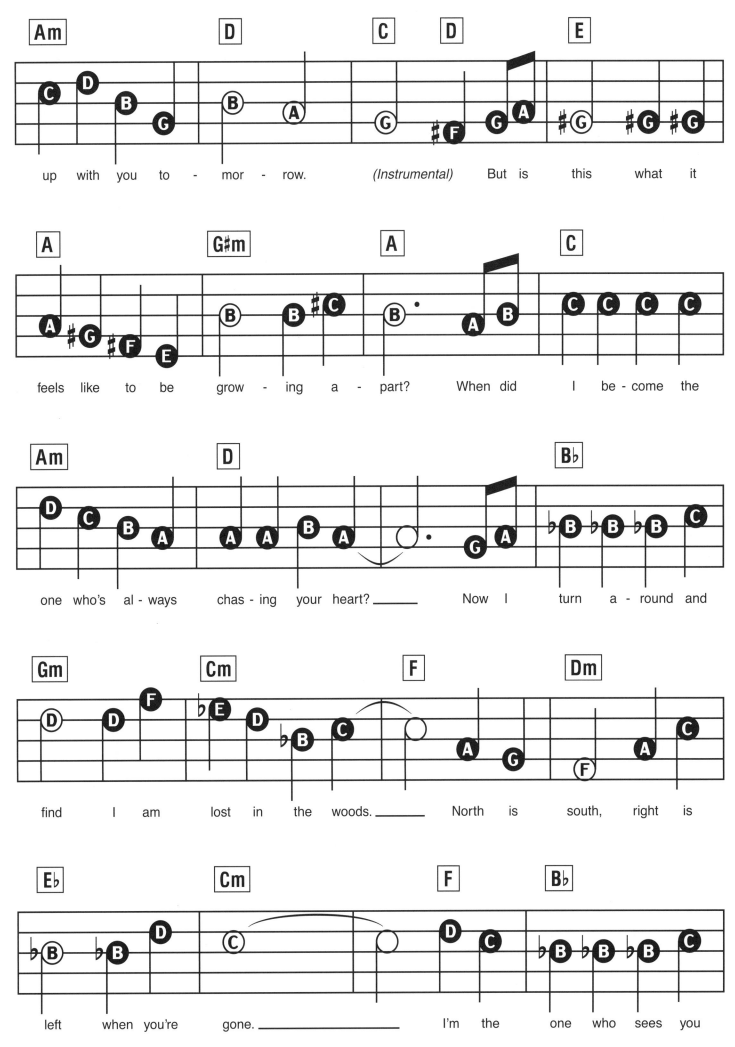

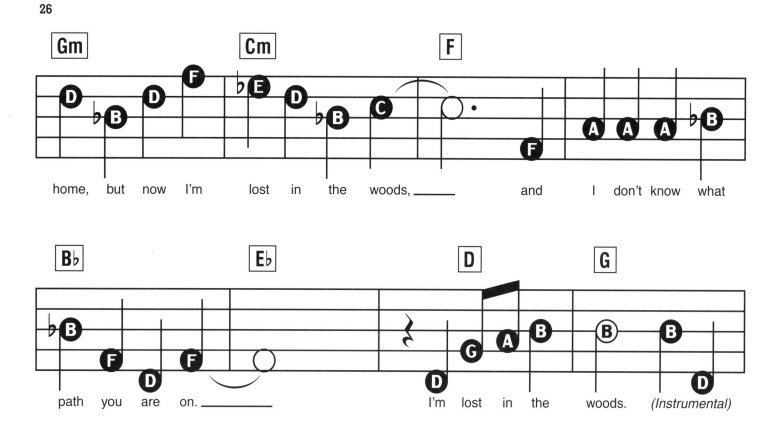

home, but now I'm lost in the woods, _____ and I don't know what

path you are on. _____ I'm lost in the woods. *(Instrumental)*

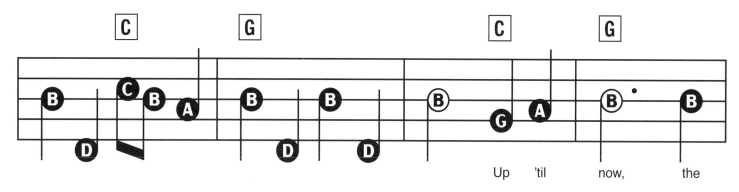

Up 'til now, the

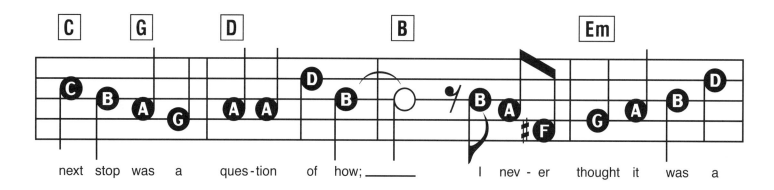

next stop was a ques-tion of how; _____ I nev-er thought it was a

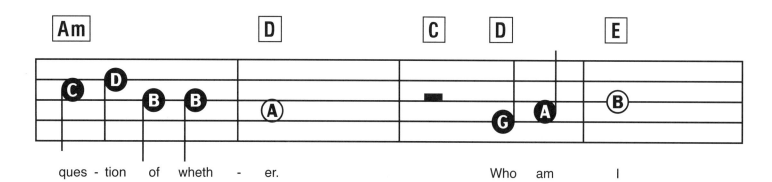

ques-tion of wheth-er. Who am I

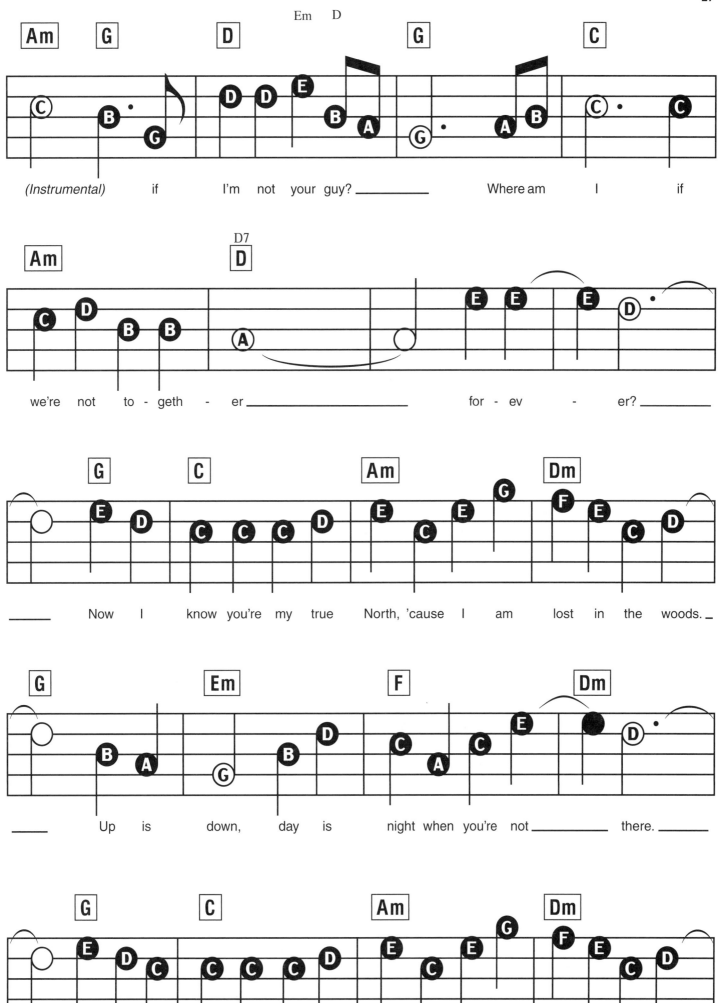

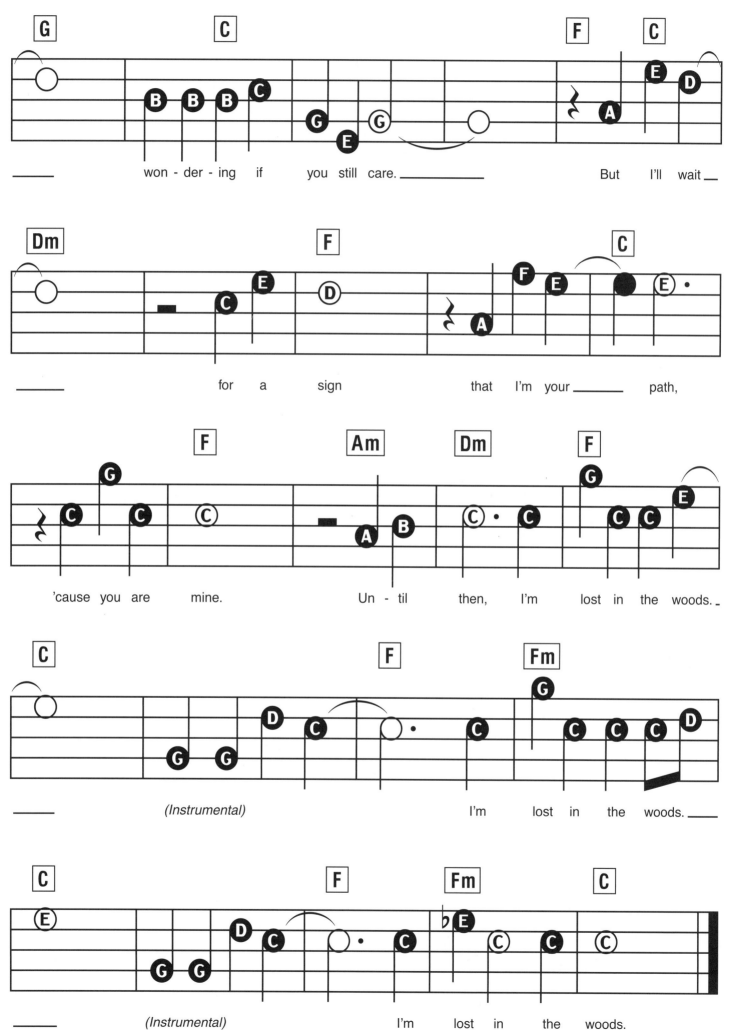

Show Yourself

Registration 4
Rhythm: Pop or Rock

Music and Lyrics by Kristen Anderson-Lopez
and Robert Lopez

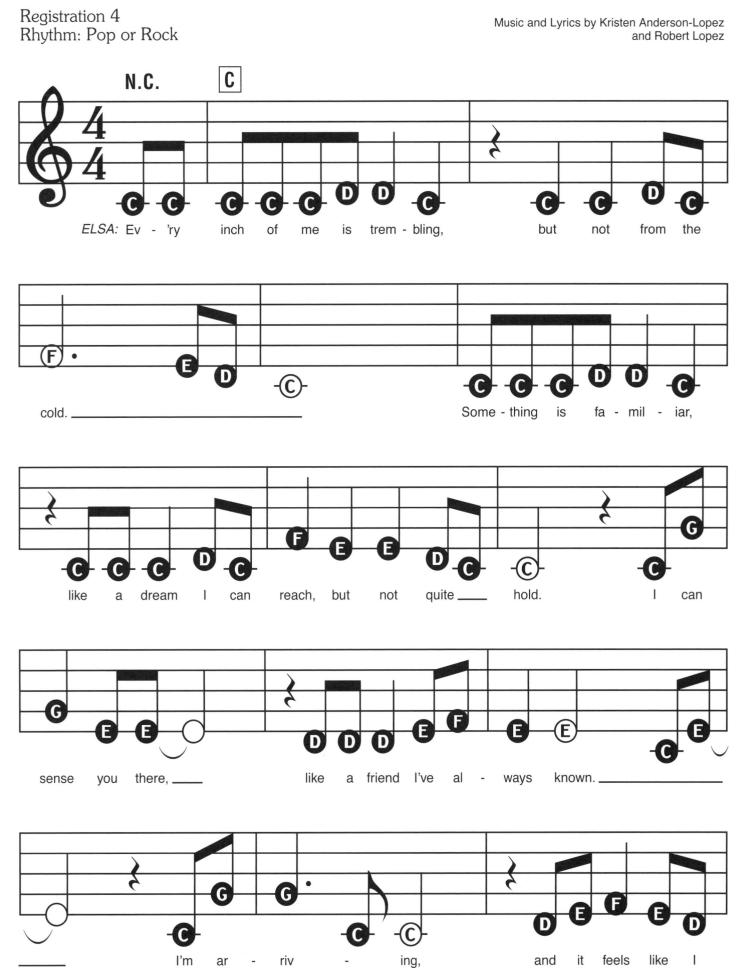

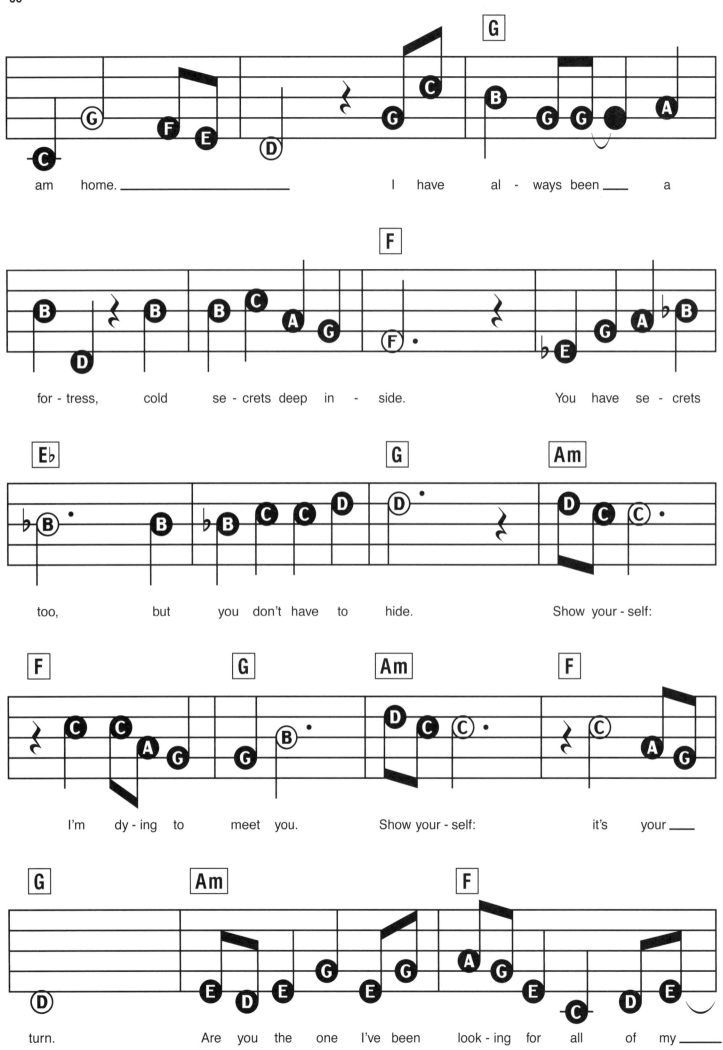

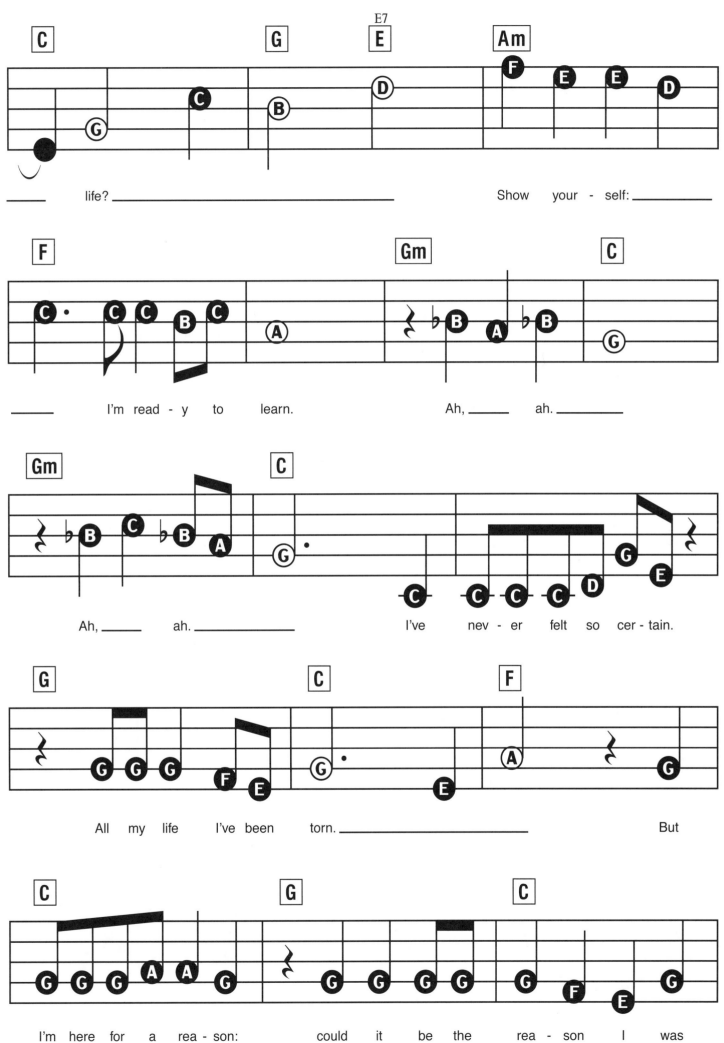

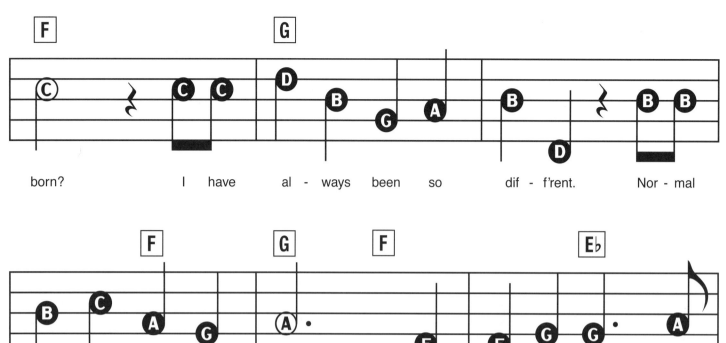

born?   I have   al - ways   been   so   dif - f'rent.   Nor - mal

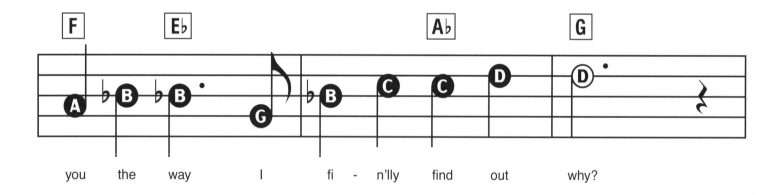

rules   did   not   ap -   ply.   Is   this   the   day?   Are

you   the   way   I   fi - n'lly   find   out   why?

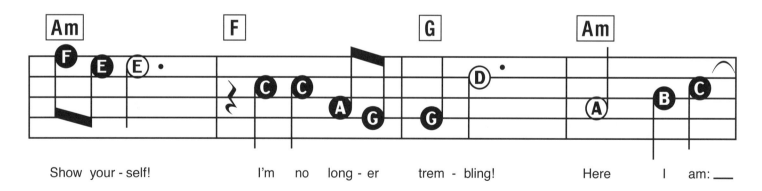

Show your - self!   I'm   no   long - er   trem - bling!   Here   I   am: __

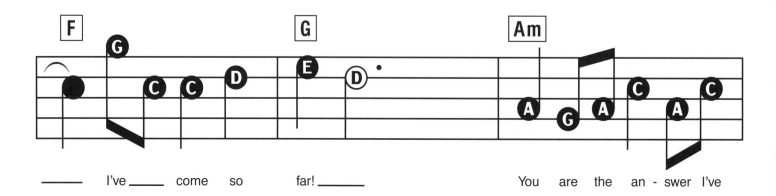

__ I've __ come so   far! _____   You   are   the   an - swer   I've

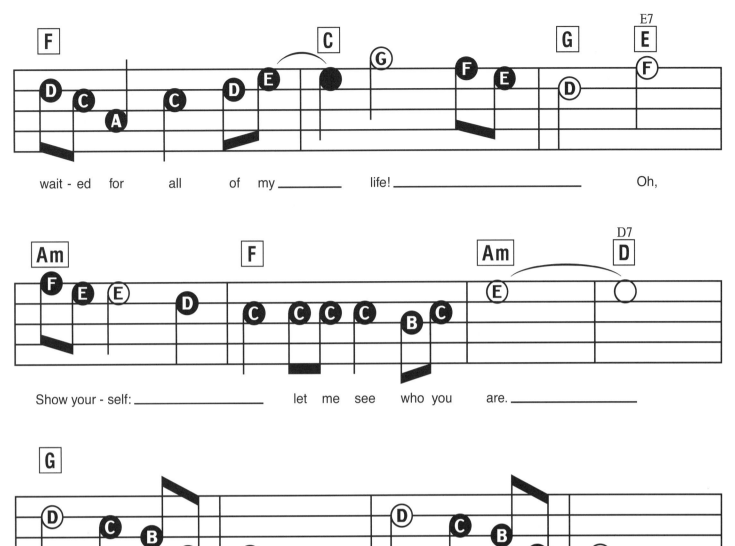

wait - ed for all of my _____ life! _____ Oh,

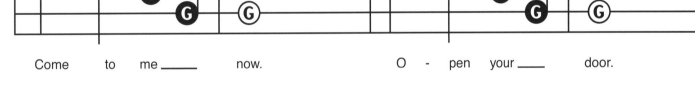

Show your - self: _____ let me see who you are. _____

Come to me _____ now. O - pen your _____ door.

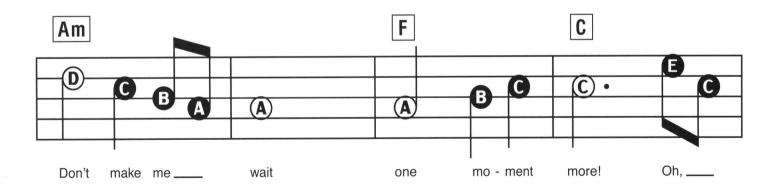

Don't make me _____ wait one mo - ment more! Oh, _____

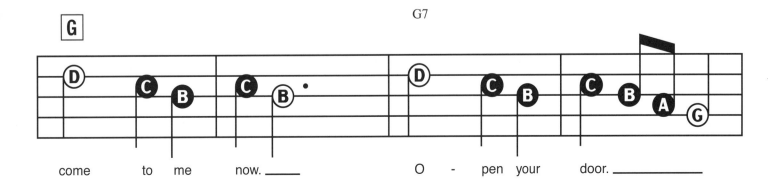

come to me now. _____ O - pen your door. _____

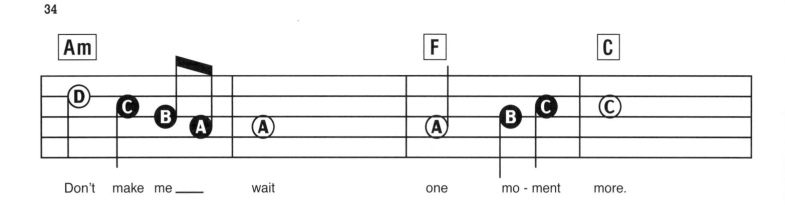

Don't make me ___ wait   one mo - ment more.

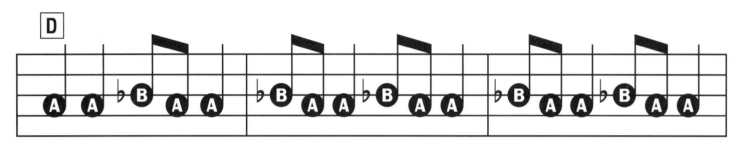

(Instrumental)

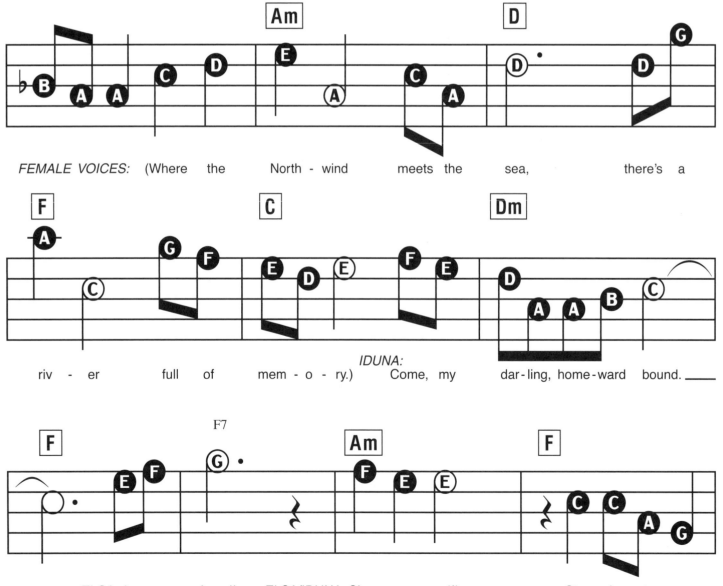

FEMALE VOICES: (Where the North - wind meets the sea, there's a

riv - er full of mem - o - ry.) Come, my dar - ling, home - ward bound. ___

___ ELSA: I am found! ELSA/IDUNA: Show your - self!   Step in - to your

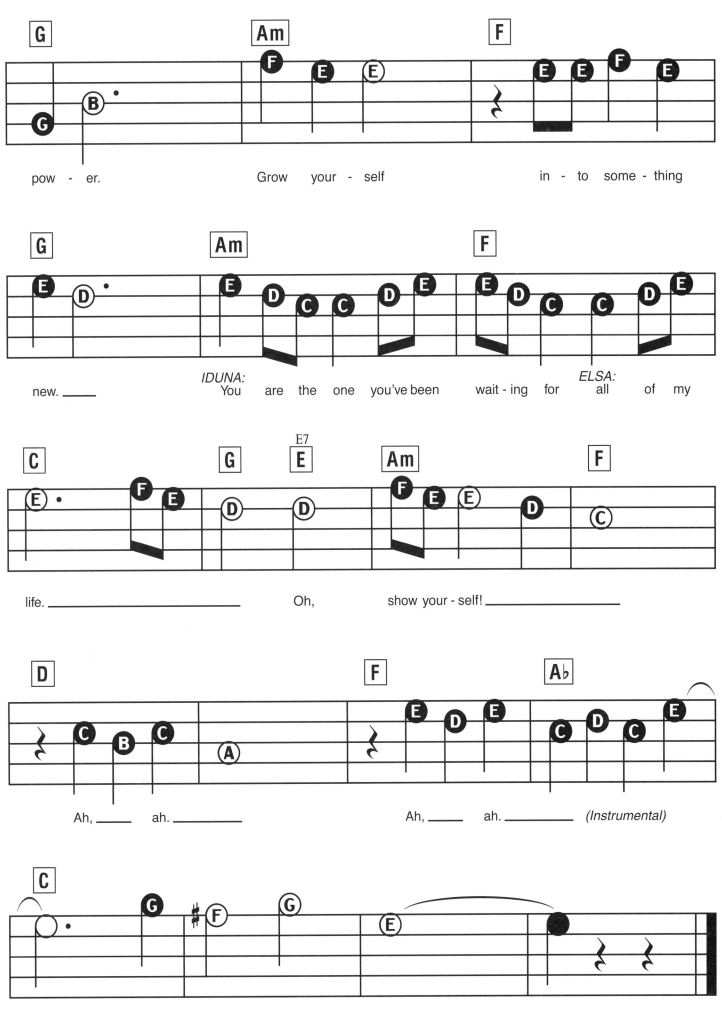

The Next Right Thing

Registration 3
Rhythm: Ballad

Music and Lyrics by Kristen Anderson-Lopez
and Robert Lopez

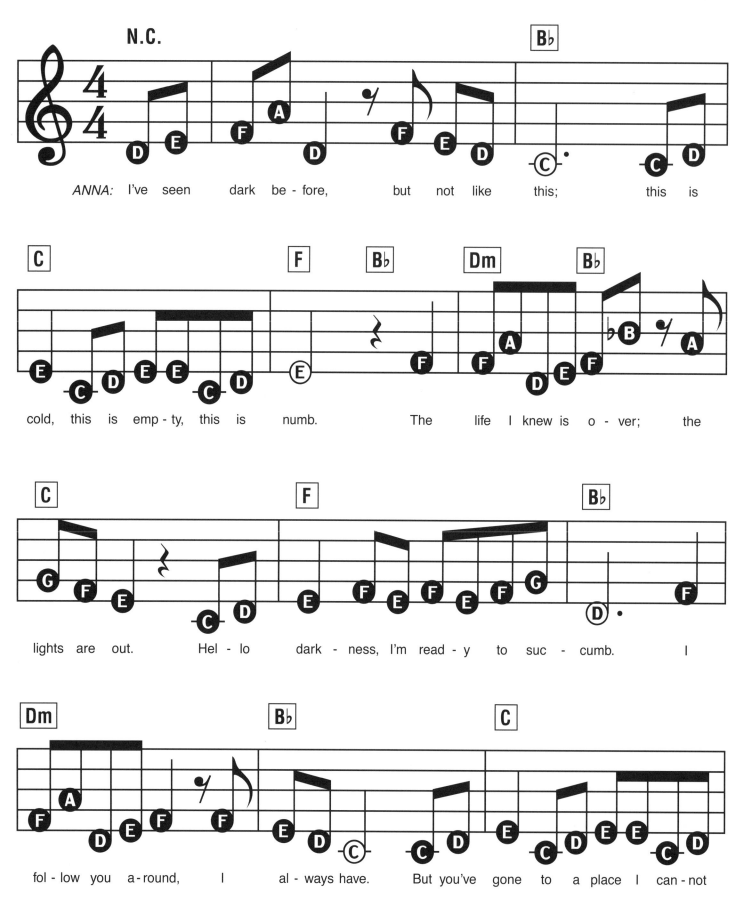

37

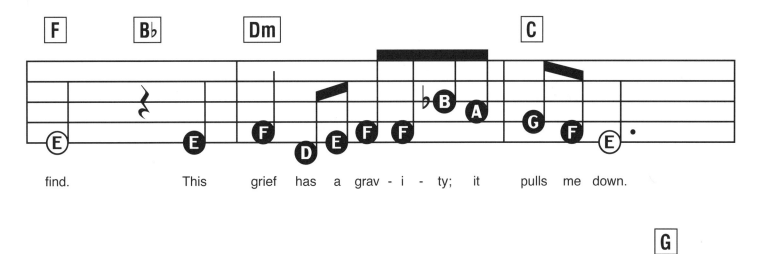

find.   This grief has a grav-i-ty; it pulls me down.

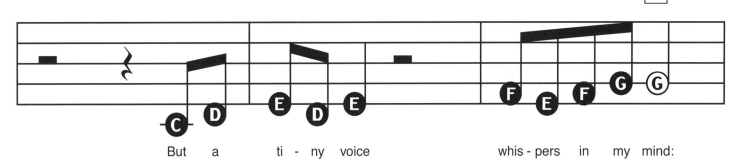

But a ti-ny voice whis-pers in my mind:

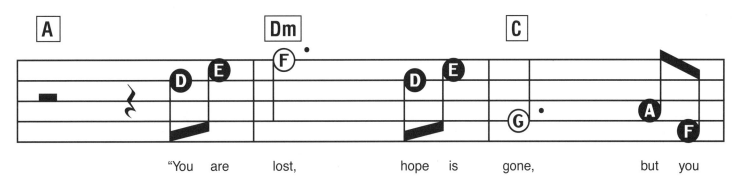

"You are lost, hope is gone, but you

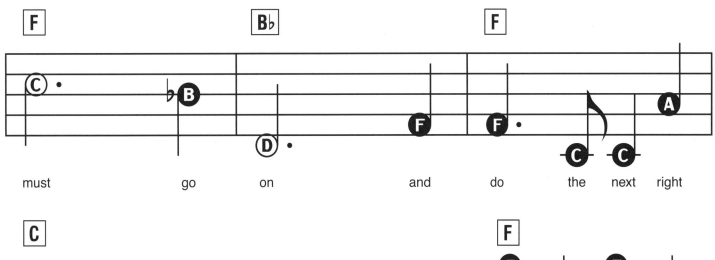

must go on and do the next right

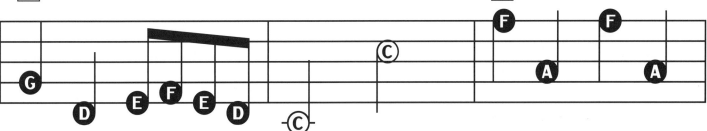

thing." *(Instrumental)*

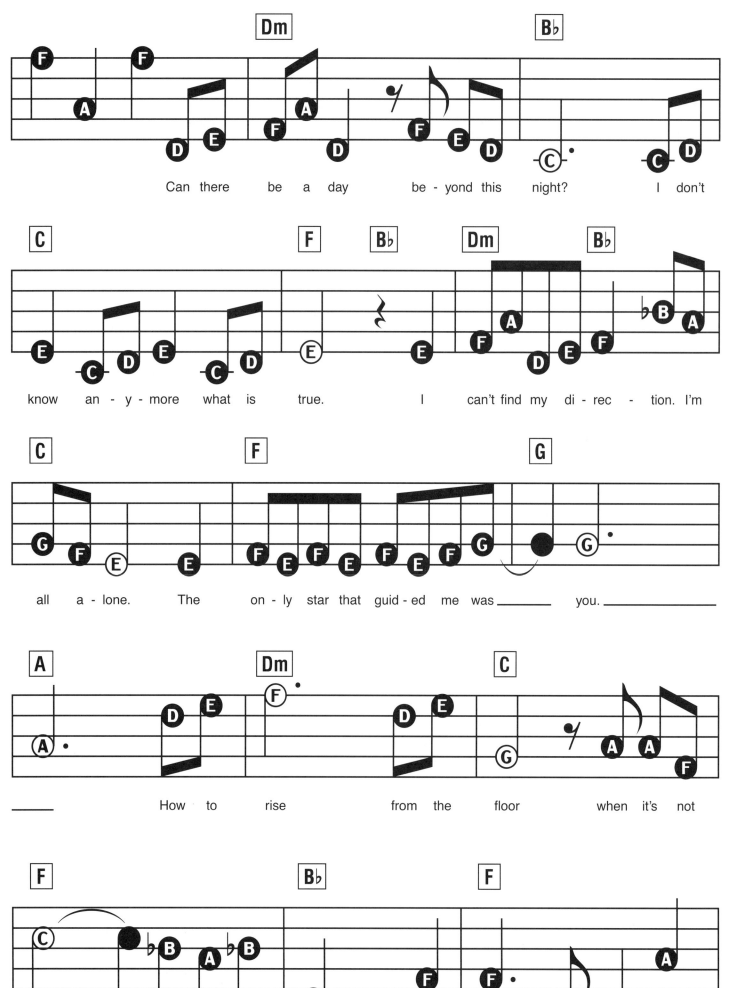

Can there be a day be-yond this night? I don't
know an-y-more what is true. I can't find my di-rec-tion. I'm
all a-lone. The on-ly star that guid-ed me was _____ you. _____
_____ How to rise from the floor when it's not
you _____ I'm ris-ing for? Just do the next right

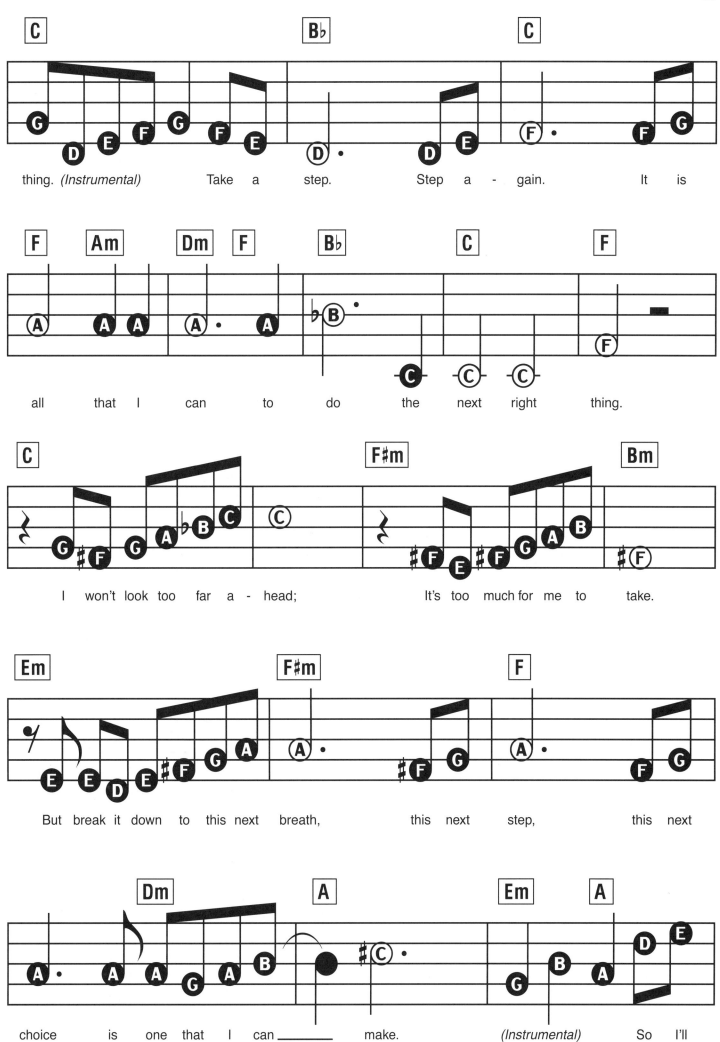

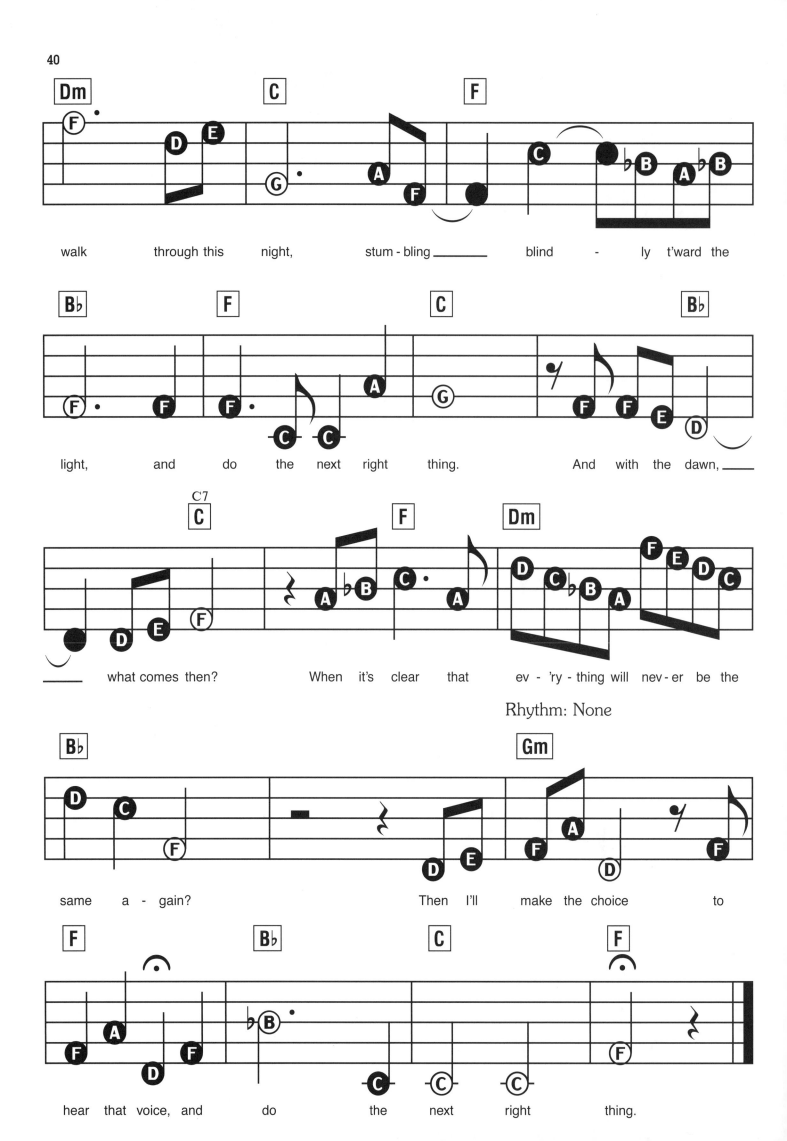